How to use this book

The Trees. All our native trees are included, as are the most common of those that have been introduced into our parks and gardens from abroad. In all, 125 species and varieties are illustrated in colour.

The Introduction. Begin by reading this. It tells you where trees grow and explains the different parts – leaves, flowers, buds, shoots and so on – that can be used for identifying trees.

The illustrated contents key shows typical members of each group of trees. Select the one most like the tree you wish to identify and turn to the relevant pages.

The Illustrations. The superb colour paintings show the complete tree, as well as details of bark, leaves, flowers and fruit where necessary. The trees are shown in their natural environments. Remember that the shape of a tree may alter according to its situation: a specimen in open parkland will often be taller and more spreading than one competing with other trees in woodland. The illustrations are of mature trees.

Hints for tree identification. The leaf is the first thing to turn to. The under side of a leaf gives more information than the upper, for the variations there in colour and hairiness are often the best way to distinguish between species with leaves of similar shapes. Leaves can still be used in winter. However bare the tree, there will be some leaves in the surrounding grass. After a little practice in summer, the bark, particularly, and the shoots and buds, can nearly always identify a tree. Fruit or remains of fruit can also be helpful.

Crown shape is independent of time of year and is enough to identify most Poplars and Elms, and is useful in Birches, Cypresses and other groups.

The more you look at trees, the more distinguishable they become. You absorb the details unconsciously. Sycamore and Norway Maple may seem alike to you now. After one year's tree-watching they will be instantly separable from a distance and you will wonder how it could ever have been otherwise.

A HANDGUIDE TO THE

TREES

OF BRITAIN AND NORTHERN EUROPE

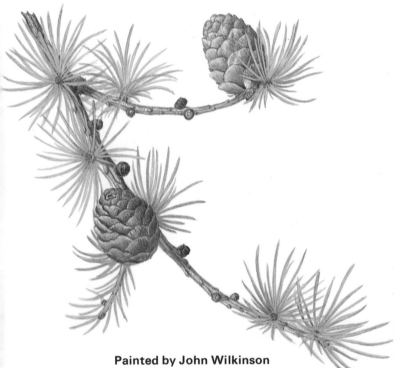

Painted by John Wilkinson

Text by Alan Mitchell

TREASURE PRESS

ACKNOWLEDGEMENTS

This title first appeared as the *Collins Handguide to the Trees of Britain and Northern Europe* and Treasure Press gratefully acknowledge the co-operation of William Collins Sons & Co Ltd who gave permission for this edition to be published.

First published in Great Britain in 1978 by William Collins Sons & Co Ltd

This edition published in 1985 by
Treasure Press
59 Grosvenor Street
London W1

Reprinted 1988

ISBN 1 85051 049 0

Printed in Portugal by Oficinas Gráficas ASA

Contents

The trees shown here are commonly seen members of their groups. Some groups, like cypresses and poplars, also contain trees of very different shapes. The illustrations below are of mature specimens grown in the open. They are not shown in scale with each other.

Maidenhair, Yews
14, 15

Firs 16

Monkey
Puzzle 18

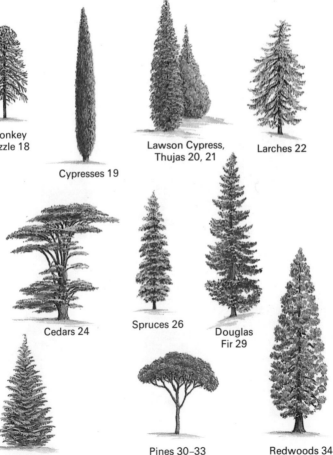

Cypresses 19

Lawson Cypress,
Thujas 20, 21

Larches 22

Cedars 24

Spruces 26

Douglas
Fir 29

Hemlocks 28

Pines 30–33

Redwoods 34

3

Willows 36

Poplars 38–41

Walnuts 42

Sweet Chestnut 43

Alder 44

Birches 45

Beech 46

Hornbeam 43

Oaks 50–53

Elms 54–57

Planes 60

Tupelo 58

4

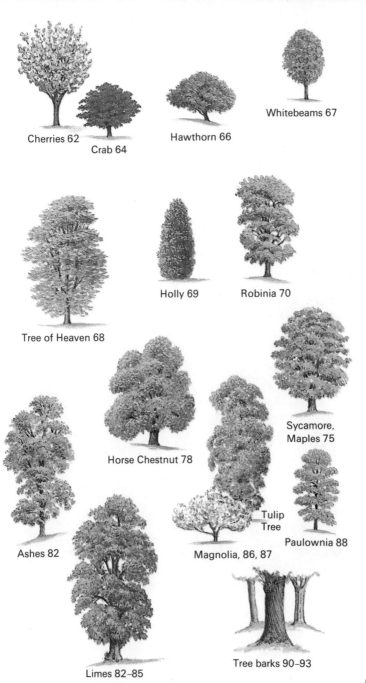

Introduction

WHAT IS A TREE? Trees are the tallest, biggest and longest-lived of all plants. The Giant Bamboo, which is not a tree but a grass, can grow to 30m (in a few weeks), and some seaweeds and climbers can be *longer* than that, but only a tree can exceed 30m in height. A tree is a perennial woody plant which can grow at least 6m on a single stem. If unable to reach 6m, or not confined to one stem, we call the plant a shrub. Trees are not a separate botanical class, but a form of growth found in many different families of plants, which may include different forms. For example, most conifers and most members of the oak/beech and poplar families are trees, though some are low shrubs; whereas the rose and the pea families include a variety of herbs and shrubs and trees. Trees are divided into *conifers* and *broadleaves*.

CONIFERS are a relatively primitive group, nearly all evergreen and with hard, mostly narrow leaves. They have separate male and female flowers, without petals. The seeds lie open on a scale, in a structure which ripens to a woody cone or may resemble a berry. The wood has no fibres, so for its strength has to rely on the sap conducting cells, which are narrow and thick-walled. The central stem dominates the growth, so that conifers include the tallest trees.

BROADLEAFED TREES are less ancient plants, with network veins allowing a great variety of leaf shapes. Outside the tropics most shed their leaves in winter. Some flowers have showy petals and some are combined male and female. The wood has fibres, which allows the vessels to be wide sap-conductors without strength. The central stem usually divides into many equally strong branches which form a domed crown.

Beech

Silver Birch

ROOTS AND TRUNK The *feeding* roots stay within 25cm of the ground surface over a wide area. But near the bole *sinker* roots may go down to various depths to give stability. On dry soils trees like beech send roots far down through the subsoil and rocks beneath to reach water, though no tree roots can grow into soil which is always saturated. Only the newest part of the root – that just behind the growing tip – has hairs and can feed. Root growth stops in November and starts again before the buds open.

Trunks grow into the shapes best able to hold their crown against wind. So in conifers with small branches and narrow crowns the boles taper gently to a great height, while in oaks with their heavy low branches the bole is stout and scarcely tapered below the branches.

TREE SHAPES are set by the height at which the central stem divides, and by the length and angle of the branches. Broadleaves tend to have the more upright branching, but in conifers the branches are level with the youngest and so shortest at the top, which produces slender, conic crowns. Sometimes a single specimen of a tree occurs with tightly upright branches, making a slender column. These are multiplied by cuttings or grafting; so we have the Lombardy Poplar, Dawyck Beech and others. Similarly, long pendulous forms with weeping crowns have been found of wych elm, ash and other trees.

WOOD Woody plants are enclosed from shoot-tip to root-tip in a layer of cells called cambium, which moves outwards with each year's growth. Below this are the cells which conduct the sap from the roots to the leaves. They live for about 20 years, then solidify to make the heartwood that gives strength to a tree. Each year the first cells made are big and thin-walled, but the last are small with thick walls; they change as a new 'ring' is made each year. Other cells in rows radiating from the centre, 'medullary rays', store food for the energy needed to make the spring growth before a deciduous tree has leaves to manufacture food. Outside the cambium, other cells in the inner bark conduct food made by the leaves down to the roots.

bark

inner bark

cambium

annual rings

medullary ray

heartwood

SHOOTS In a tree a shoot is an annual extension of permanent growth, bearing flowers or leaves directly. Where it ends in a flower it will extend no further. Nearly all shoot growth occurs in May and June in a rapid burst, all growth being a new addition, not a lengthening of a previous year's shoot. By branching every year, and with each side-shoot again branching in the following year, the crowns of trees like oak and birch would soon become impossibly dense. So many side-shoots stop, die, and are shed during the summer.

Sycamore

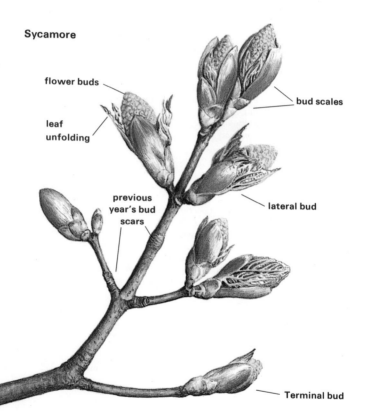

flower buds

bud scales

leaf unfolding

previous year's bud scars

lateral bud

Terminal bud

BUDS are of three kinds. The smallest contain only one leaf or a pair; bigger buds hold the next year's shoots; and the biggest of all contain the flowers. In most trees the next year's shoots and flowers fill the buds by July. Most buds are protected by hard or hairy *bud-scales*, though in a few trees the folded leaves are naked. Cypresses and eucalyptus rest between the growth periods without any buds at all. The scales of shoot-buds often leave scars, which show the annual growth.

Larch ♂ ♀
♂ Alder Oak ♂ Elm ♂♀
Almond ♂♀

FLOWERS In all conifers and catkin-bearing broadleafed trees the male flowers are separate from the female ones and very different. The male flowers have only to produce pollen which the wind then takes to the female. In most petalled flowers the two are combined, with male stamens surrounding the female style, and pollination is done mainly by insects. But in some trees with petalled flowers, as in the hollies, the male and female flowers are on separate trees.

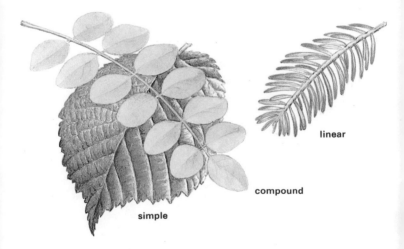

linear

compound

simple

LEAVES are the working part of a tree, drawing the sap up from the roots and using it with the energy from light to make the food for the tree and its growth. They are therefore arranged on the shoot to catch the maximum of light. Evergreen leaves stay active on the tree for from three to ten or more years and are shed when they die, usually in summer. Single leaves may be up to 50cm, but the biggest leaves are compound – those made up of many leaflets on a single central stalk, falling with it in autumn.

THE TREES IN THIS BOOK Although there are far too many kinds of trees for any book like this to be 'complete' we have tried to include all the important and common trees, and also some which are much less common but which are likely to be noticed. There should be no countryside tree that is not in the book – if it really is a tree and not a shrub, we do not include shrubs – and very few of those found in city parks, squares, churchyards or small gardens will be missing. It is in botanical gardens and big tree collections that you will find many trees which we have omitted to keep this book small and light.

WHERE TREES LIVE Trees are found growing from sea-level to 4000m up in the Himalaya; from the Equator to the edge of the tundra; from rainforests with 5000mm of annual rainfall to deserts. Rainfall itself is less important than the water which may be obtained from the ground: palms flourish in some places where it may rain only once in five years, provided they have access to underground water. Towards the Pole and up a mountain trees are limited by the shortness of the available growing season: plant growth needs a temperature of at least 5°C. and trees need some two months mostly well above this to complete their growth.

Many trees are adapted to growing in permanent swamp and even in brackish and salt water, but they cannot overcome complete drought.

Poplar   Silver Fir   Lime   Oak   Yew

AGE In general, trees which grow very fast have a short life-span. Willows and poplars, for instance, rapidly make big trees which become senile and decay in a hundred years: a birch may die of old age at sixty. Trees like Silver Firs with a slow start but then a period of rapid growth tend to live for about 200 years. Limes and oaks grow first at moderate rates, then slowly, to survive 400–500 years. Yews are very slow and their wood exceedingly strong, so they can hold together even when very hollow for well over 1000 years.

NATIVE TREES For about a million years northern Europe underwent the Ice Ages. But since the mountain chains of central and southern Europe run east and west they formed a barrier to southward migration by trees, and though there were certain refuges a great many species became extinct. Some sixty kinds of tree survived. Of these thirty-five, including three conifers, managed to recolonise the British Isles before the English Channel separated us from the mainland. Today native trees still dominate the countryside but towns, gardens and parks now have more trees from China, Japan and North America.

WHY TREES ARE IMPORTANT They are an essential element in all types of scenery – except cliff and mountain-top. In cities they give us shade, shelter, colour and seasonal change; in gardens they add the dimension of height as well as a great variety of foliage, flowers, fruit and bark. More important still, trees make and retain rich soils. Their roots go deeper and bring up minerals beyond the reach of other plants. These the decaying leaves spread upon the surface, where they are broken down by bacteria and fungi to form the humus layer needed by plant roots. Trees also circulate oxygen by freeing it from the carbon dioxide in the air to use the carbon in making wood. But as the wood later rots in the forest the carbon turns back to carbon monoxide, so there is no net gain in oxygen.

oxygen, water vapour

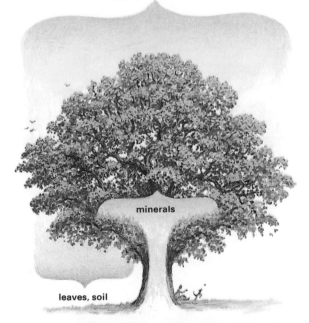

minerals

leaves, soil

13

MAIDENHAIR TREE *(Ginkgo biloba)* from China is the only survivor of an ancient plant group quite unrelated to conifers and other modern plants. It thrives where summers are warm, even in city streets among skyscrapers and is much planted also in parks and gardens. Arising before network vein systems evolved, the broad leaves are shaped by the primitive fan-like veining. They unfold bright green in April and turn clear gold in autumn. Each tree is either male or female. Males are much more commonly planted, and may when old bear thick yellow catkins. The rare female trees bear clusters of fruit like small yellow plums, ripening brown. Young trees may grow 60cm in one year, nothing at all during the following two, then 60cm again the year after.

YEW *(Taxus baccata)* is one of the strongest and most durable timbers. This allows a tree, although very hollow, to live on until it is a thousand years old or more, still supporting heavy branches. Such trees can be 3m through. This tree is wild on chalk and limestone hills and in oakwoods throughout Europe. The bark is pale red-brown and purplish, falling in large flakes. Male trees bear small pale yellow flowers beneath the shoots and shed clouds of pollen in February. Female trees have tiny green flowers which ripen into fleshy scarlet cups around black, highly poisonous seeds. The foliage, fresh or dried is also poisonous to many animals. Yew will grow in some shade and clips well to make a very robust hedge. The upright **Irish Yew ('Fastigiata')**, common in churchyards, is a female with leaves spiralled around the shoot. Every plant of this form derives originally from one found wild in Northern Ireland in 1790.

Irish Yew

YEW

SILVER FIR *(Abies alba)* grows on the ◁ Alps and nearby mountains and is planted in forests and gardens. The leaf underside has two silver bands but the tree is named from its bark. The cones are borne only near the top of old trees and break up leaving the central spike on the branch. Very slow growth can be made for many years in deep shade, and then when given light the tree may make shoots of 80cm and can be more than 50m tall.

GRAND FIR *(Abies grandis)* is like the ◁ Silver Fir but has shinier, brighter green, longer leaves and grows even faster. Sent in 1831 from Pacific North America where it is often 70m tall, it can be 50m in 80 years in Britain. The small buds are purple. Bruised leaves are strongly scented of oranges. Cones are borne only around the tips of trees more than 50 years old, so are seldom seen from the ground.

NOBLE FIR *(Abies procera)* is from ◁ Oregon and Washington and is as big there as the Grand Fir. It is distinct in its blue upcurved small leaves the same colour each side and the big cones freely borne even on some young trees. It is planted in some western mountain forests and in many gardens. Male flowers are big crimson globules along the underside of shoots; females are erect from upper shoots, 5cm, yellow, with finely pointed bracts. The silvery-grey bark may become dark purple with age, or crack into dull grey plates. Young trees have neat conic crowns.

SILVER FIR

GRAND FIR

NOBLE FIR

MONKEY PUZZLE

GOLDEN CHINESE JUNIPER

MONKEY PUZZLE *(Araucaria araucana)* grows in the
◁ southern Andes and was brought from Chile in 1796. It is
a poor tree near cities but luxuriant near west coasts and
withstands strong winds. The foliage is rather unfriendly,
each triangular leaf being hard and spine-tipped. Male
trees bear stout catkins several at the end of a shoot and
females have erect, globular, 15cm cones which are
green but have golden spines.

GOLDEN CHINESE JUNIPER (*Juniperus chinensis*
◁ 'Aurea') arose in 1855 in a nursery in Surrey, England,
among normal seedlings. It grows well in towns. The
colour is enhanced by yellow male flowers profusely
borne from midsummer until April.

SMOOTH ARIZONA CYPRESS

ITALIAN CYPRESS *(Cupressus sempervirens)* in the wild has level branches, but this fastigiate form is the one most planted. The foliage is almost scentless when crushed, but the wood is prized for its pleasant aroma which repels the clothes moth and so is used for chests and wardrobes.

SMOOTH ARIZONA CYPRESS *(Cupressus glabra)* endures heat, drought and frost and is a shapely blue-grey tree with dark purple bark flaking to leave yellow and red patches. When crushed the foliage has the scent of grapefruit. Clusters of dark purple cones stay on the tree for years.

19

'Lutea'

'Erecta'

'Ellwoodii'

△

LAWSON CYPRESS *(Chamaecyparis lawsoniana)* is wild only in small areas near the Oregon-California boundary, where it is uniformly sea-green. Sent to Britain in 1854, it had by 1855 produced the bright green upright form **'Erecta'**. Since then, in nurseries in Britain and the Netherlands, it has given a profusion of forms of diverse colours, habit and stature now grown widely in Europe and back in the USA. **'Lutea'** was the first good golden form (1873) and **'Ellwoodii'** is semi-dwarf upright and dark grey. The foliage when crushed has a parsley scent. Myriads of tiny crimson male flowers tip each spray in spring; the dark grey female flowers are a little back on the shoots. Cones are abundant, globular, 7mm across often blue-grey in summer. The scent in the foliage, and the tree's drooping tip, occur in all the many forms of Lawson Cypress.

WESTERN RED CEDAR *(Thuja plicata)* is not a true cedar but a kind of cypress found from Alaska to California. It grows rapidly in mild wet western areas to 30m, but is slow in dry places. It is often grown as a hedge, clipping well, and is a useful forest tree to grow in the shade of old larch woods, giving a light, strong timber. The foliage is brighter green and shinier than that of Lawson Cypress and is strongly fragrant of pineapple. Male flowers are inconspicuous and briefly yellow at the tips of the foliage, shedding pollen in March. The cones behind the tips are leathery, 1cm long and yellow turning brown. The bark is dark red-brown and falls away in long thin strips. **Golden-barred Thuja ('Zebrina')** has the foliage broadly but variably banded bright yellow and can be a splendid golden specimen already 25m tall.

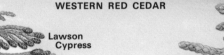

WESTERN RED CEDAR

'Zebrina'

Lawson Cypress

21

JAPANESE LARCH

EUROPEAN LARCH

22

JAPANESE LARCH *(Larix kaempferi)*
is more robust than the European ▷
larch, broader when young and with
more shoots, which are dark orange.
The broader leaves are grey beneath
and the female flowers are cream and
red. The cones, often densely borne,
are short with the scales bent down at
the tips. The tree can grow 20m in 20
years and is planted in forests for a
quick crop of strong timber.

Japanese

HYBRID LARCH *(Larix × eurolepis)*
is a cross between Japanese and ▷
European and is a good mixture of
them, but usually of faster growth and
bearing more cones. These have
scales turned out but not down. The
shoots are orange and the female
flowers are big and pink, white,
yellow or green.

Hybrid

EUROPEAN LARCH *(Larix decidua)*
is wild from the Alps to Poland and ▷
has been planted in forests and gardens everywhere. Its bright new
leaves are welcome in early spring
and it turns gold in late autumn. It
grows very fast and attracts many
kinds of birds.

European

CEDAR OF LEBANON *(Cedrus libani)*. Many trees are called "cedars" but the three in this picture are the true Cedars. The Lebanon Cedar grows fast from a slender young tree to a majestic spreading specimen. Few in gardens are yet 180 years old. Male flowers stand all summer, like 5cm green cones, and shed their pollen in late autumn.

ATLAS CEDAR *(Cedrus atlantica)*. The form nearly always seen is this blue one from one valley in Algeria. It is tolerant of drought and limestones and grows rapidly. The female flowers, only 1 cm tall, are bright green and at the centres of some of the whorls of leaves in September.

DEODAR *(Cedrus deodara)* is the cedar of the Himalaya. It is frequent in town gardens and distinct from the other cedars as it has a more slender crown, much longer needles and drooping tips to shoots and apex.

DEODAR

◁ **ATLAS CEDAR**

Δ

SITKA SPRUCE *(Picea sitchensis)* is the giant of the spruces, many within its natural range from Alaska to California being 80m tall and 3m through the bole. It is the chief forest tree in mountains near European west coasts, giving heavy crops on high wet peaty land. The flattened needles have bright white bands beneath and are hard and spiny. The tree is dark blue-grey from a distance.

NORWAY SPRUCE *(Picea abies)* is native to most of Europe, where it is a major forest tree, hardier than Sitka Spruce. The four-sided needles are green all round. The red female flowers ripen to long leathery cones. Small specimens are used in Britain for Christmas trees.

BLUE COLORADO SPRUCE *(Picea pungens* var. *glauca)*. Some blue-white forms of this are commonly planted in town gardens. In dry places they can be twiggy and thin with age but at its best it is a fine column of blue, 20m tall. The brown or orange grooved shoots bear stout, rigid and spined needles all round them. The cones are whitish, darkening with time, and appear around the top of the tree in some years.

▽

△

SERBIAN SPRUCE *(Picea omorika)*, discovered in 1876 in a remote valley in Jugoslavia, is among the best conifers for planting in towns. It has a neat, slender crown, is very hardy and tolerates almost any soils. The flat needles are broadly banded blue-white beneath. It starts to bear cones near the top when still very young.

BLUE COLORADO SPRUCE 27

EASTERN HEMLOCK   WESTERN HEMLOCK

EASTERN HEMLOCK *(Tsuga canadensis)* in its
◁ native hills is a slender tree but here it is broad
and often a big bush. The leaves taper from near
the base and a line of them lies over the shoot
with the white-banded side uppermost.

WESTERN HEMLOCK *(Tsuga heterophylla)* can
◁ be 70m tall in Washington and grows in W.
Europe at great speed to an elegant conic tree
with drooping apex. The leaves have parallel
sides. Female flowers are rosy purple.

DOUGLAS FIR *(Pseudotsuga menziesii)* grows over most of the Rocky Mountain region and is one of the few trees in the world to be over 90m tall. It is a widely planted forest tree in Europe yielding huge amounts of strong timber. The soft foliage has a powerful fruity scent. The slender buds are unusual in conifers and the three-pronged bracts protruding from the cone are unique to Douglas Firs. The tops of old trees are often broken by strong winds, though they may often reach 45m first. Wet snow can break their branches.

MONTEREY PINE *(Pinus radiata)* is a tree wonder. The wild population is minute, in two coastal areas of California. There it is a short-lived tree to 20m tall. Watered in gardens further north it has grown 15m in five years and in New Zealand forests one grew 60m in 41 years. It has been the main timber tree of the southern hemisphere, now being replaced by some Mexican pines less given to disease. It is tender in Europe except near west coasts. The slender bright green needles are in threes. The heavy cones cling to the branches in whorls of three for thirty or more years. Where winters are very mild, it stops growing for only a month or two. Other pines stop in July and restart in May.

MONTEREY PINE

AROLLA PINE

BHUTAN PINE

BHUTAN PINE *(Pinus wallichiana)* from the western Himalaya is quite frequent in parks and even town gardens where its blue hanging needles are admired. The needles are five in a bundle. Female flowers are at the tips of new shoots, club-shaped and pink on a stalk. The cones are often numerous and may be 30cm long.

AROLLA PINE *(Pinus cembra)*, the pine of the high Alps, makes a neat dense tree. Its needles are in fives, blue-black with bright white inner surfaces and the shoot is densely covered in brown short hairs. Cones are on old trees only and in summer are deep blue.

SCOTS PINE

CORSICAN PINE

SCOTS PINE *(Pinus sylvestris)* ranges from Spain to east Siberia and yields the timber called 'deal'. The needles, in pairs, are often quite blue and the orange-red bark is a feature.

CORSICAN PINE *(Pinus nigra* var. *maritima)* is a form of Austrian Pine much superior in forestry as it is straight, tall, narrow and fast. The paired needles are long, slender and twisted, borne on pale brown shoots.

STONE PINE

Δ

AUSTRIAN PINE *(Pinus nigra nigra)* is a rugged dark form, often heavily branched and of little use in forestry but valuable as shelter-tree on exposed limestone hills.

STONE PINE *(Pinus pinea)*. The broad parasol crowns of this, the 'Umbrella Pine' are common on Mediterranean shores and it is planted sparingly much further north. The big seeds in the heavy cone are ground to make flour.

33

GIANT SEQUOIA

◁ **COAST REDWOOD** *(Sequoia sempervirens)* grows in the fog-belt by the coast of N. California, where a tree 112m tall is the tallest in the world. Since 1850 it has become common in Western Europe but is scorched by dry cold winds and attains 40m only in damp sheltered places. The egg-shaped cone is only 2cm long, wrinkled and spined.

Coast Redwood

GIANT SEQUOIA *(Sequoiadendron*
◁ *giganteum),* or 'Wellingtonia', the
world's bulkiest tree, was found in in-
terior California in 1852 and is now
common in Europe. It has thick, spongy
bark and hard cords of foliage scented
of aniseed. The globular cones are 3cm
across. Each shoot-tip can bear a small
whitish male flower.

DAWN REDWOOD   SWAMP CYPRESS

DAWN REDWOOD *(Metasequoia glyptostroboides)* known only as a fossil
until 1941 was then found growing in China. Now in most big parks and
gardens it will grow more than a metre a year on a warm damp site. The
leaves and shoots are in opposite pairs and fall together in the autumn.

SWAMP CYPRESS *(Taxodium distichum)* inhabits coastal and riverine
swamps of eastern USA. The leaves, set spirally like the shoots, are more
slender and numerous than those of Dawn Redwood, and unfold much
later. Short post-like growths or 'knees' arise from the root in wet soils.

CRACK
WILLOW

WHITE
WILLOW

CRACK WILLOW *(Salix fragilis)* is the most frequent riverside willow in big valleys. Formerly it was often pollarded and most trees bush out from 2m up a stout bole – to which point they were periodically cut back. The glossy rich green leaves are the biggest of any common willow. A shoot bent back somewhat will snap cleanly away at the base: hence the name.

WHITE WILLOW *(Salix alba)* is tall and narrow as a young tree, growing fast. It has slender shoots which are pinkish-grey and densely covered in short hairs.

WEEPING WILLOW

SALLOW

CORAL-BARK WILLOW (*Salix* 'Cher-mesina') is a form of White Willow aris-ing in Germany in 1840. Young shoots are bright orange-red in winter and trees may be cut back every few years to give long colourful shoots.

WEEPING WILLOW (*Salix* 'Tristis' or ✕ *chrysocoma*) is either a form of White Willow or a hybrid between that and the Chinese 'Babylon Willow' (which has brown shoots and is grown only in warm countries). This form has pale yellow shoots brightest in spring and comes into leaf early. It usually bears only male flowers, curved, slender, yel-low, 8cm long.

SALLOW (*Salix caprea*) or Pussy Willow is common in damp woods or on heaths and rough ground. It is usually bushy but can be a rather upright tree of 15m.

♀   ♂

37

EUROPEAN BLACK POPLAR *(Populus nigra)* is now seldom planted but broad old trees with burry boles grow in valley woods. Long ago the American Cottonwood was sent to Europe, crossed with this poplar and gave hybrids which are preferred for their faster, cleaner growth.

BLACK ITALIAN POPLAR *(Populus* 'Serotina'*)* is an early one of these hybrids common in lowland valleys, a male tree always, profusely hung with dark red catkins in March. The leaves are very late to unfold – pale orange in late May, then greyish-green.

BLACK POPLAR   BLACK ITALIAN POPLAR

Populus 'Robusta' is a more recent hybrid of immense vigour which can grow 2.5m a year when young. It has prominent rich red male catkins and its new leaves are bright orange. A neat conic tree with uncurved branches.

LOMBARDY POPLAR (*Populus nigra* 'Italica') is a form of Black Poplar spread from Turin after 1750, and planted extensively. This form is always male and the dark red catkins are borne in the upper crown.

Robusta'

LOMBARDY POPLAR

WHITE POPLAR *(Populus alba)* has its shoot, leaf-stalks and underside densely felted white. As the buds unfold it shimmers silver against a dark sky. Later the top of the leaf turns dark green. Male trees have short purplish-grey catkins while those on females are green with small fruit which bear white tufts of wool before they fall in early summer. Thickets of suckers often grow up around the trees and make useful shelter against seawinds blowing sand on to a coast.

ASPEN

△
GREY POPLAR *(Populus canescens)* is in some features between Aspen and White poplar but is a much bigger, more robust tree than either. Nearly all the trees seen are male with grey-purple catkins in early spring.

ASPEN *(Populus tremula)* wood makes the best matches, not breaking when struck. A small suckering tree with smooth pale grey bark, its leaves flutter readily on their slender, flattened stalks, and by northern streams they turn clear yellow in the autumn.

WALNUT

BLACK
WALNUT

SWEET
CHESTNUT

SWEET CHESTNUT *(Castanea sativa)* was spread well to the north from south Europe by the Romans. Strong young shoots are dark purple and ridged. Dense bunches of cream-white male catkins open in June.

WALNUT *(Juglans regia)*, long planted widely for its fruit, came from SE Europe and from Asia. The leaves emerge orange-brown slowly fading through pale brown to dark yellowish-green. It is the only walnut with smooth leaflet-margins.

BLACK WALNUT *(Juglans nigra)* from eastern N. America is named from the dark, deeply ridged bark and makes a fine tall tree in warm areas. The leaves open yellow-green, soon turning bright shiny green, and may bear 23 toothed leaflets. The big fruit have a strong sweet scent when scratched.

ALDER *(Alnus glutinosa)* is common everywhere by fresh water. Perhaps because used to the wet, its wood stands much wetting and drying so was used for mill-clogs and canal-locks, but it also made good gunpowder charcoal. Male catkins open very early and the little dark red female flowers on the same trees ripen into cone-like woody fruit whose seeds float on water. Alder leaves remain on the tree dark green into November. The side buds on shoots have short stalks and are dark red. The bark of old trees is grey, and fissured like that of oak.

Silver Birch

Downy Birch

ALDER

SILVER BIRCH

DOWNY BIRCH

SILVER BIRCH *(Betula pendula)* grows throughout Europe to the far north on sandy or light soils and often has a weeping crown. Young plants have dark red, smooth bark and grow very fast on open sites, where it soon becomes white. The timber is strong and elastic but is now used largely in plywood.

DOWNY BIRCH *(Betula pubescens)* inhabits the same regions as the Silver Birch but in wetter poorly drained parts of heaths and on deeper peats. Its bark is less clear white and lacks the black diamond shapes. The crown is never weeping but is a confusion of curving shoots.

45

BEECH

BEECH *(Fagus sylvatica)* Beech cannot make roots in saturated soils but will drive them through dry layers to reach moisture. Hence although a thirsty tree it is not found in wet hollows nor on clays but it thrives on chalk hills and on light sandy soils. Male flowers are little balls of stamens on slender stalks and are soon shed. Female flowers are green with white filaments and are on short stout stalks. Beech live for barely 250 years, then die and fall to pieces suddenly. The timber is excellent for indoor uses like furniture. Many forms have arisen with leaves of various shades of dull red-purple. In one, the **Copper Beech** ('Purpurea') they open and remain for a few days a pale pinkish-brown. In about 1860 a strictly upright form was found in a plantation on the Scottish estate of **Dawyck** and was moved down to the garden. Grafts from this tree are now commonly planted and make a fine tree like a Lombardy Poplar. The **Weeping Beech** ('Pendula') is slender as a young tree then usually spreads widely. In some the branches root when they meet the ground and a ring of new boles surround the old.

Copper

Dawyck

Weeping

47

HORNBEAM *(Carpinus betulus)*, among the hardest and strongest of all timbers, once made mill cogwheels and hubs of cartwheels where great strength is essential, and is used for hammers in pianos. It will grow on clays too stiff for most trees. The smooth lead-grey bark is on a deeply grooved bole. Male catkins open from buds early in spring with female flowers, slender green cylinders, on nearby shoots. In autumn the leaves turn yellow and orange or russet. The tree itself is seldom planted but the **"Pyramidal Hornbeam"** (**'Fastigiata'**) is now common in streets and on roadsides, where its dense shapely crown is decorative, and colours similarly in autumn.

'Pyramidal'

HORNBEAM

RED OAK *(Quercus rubra)* was sent from eastern America more than 200 years ago. Young trees have very big leaves which turn deep red in autumn; big trees tend to show brown autumn colours. The acorns take two years to ripen

RED OAK

and are minute during their first summer. Young trees can grow as much as 1.5m in a year, and the diameter of the bole increases rapidly until old age. Red Oaks do not seem to live more than 200 years, and grow best on light soils.

ENGLISH OAK *(Quercus robur)* ranges over nearly all Europe, growing best on valley clays. A few veterans have boles 3m through, very hollow and about 800 years old. Male flowers are slender yellowish catkins from last year's buds and females are tiny green globules with red styles, at the base of leaves on the new emerging shoot. The unfolding leaves vary greatly both in time and in colour, which can be yellow or shades of brown to orange. Many kinds of tiny wasp cause galls on the leaves of most trees; the oak-apple, currant, hop and spangle-galls, and the knopper-gall – a big woody distortion of the acorn.

CYPRESS OAK *(Q.r.* 'fastigiata') is a form of English Oak with nearly erect branches. Many of those of the shape illustrated here come from a tree found near Frankfurt in Germany but acorns from this give some broader trees as well.

ENGLISH OAK

CYPRESS OAK

SESSILE OAK

SESSILE OAK *(Quercus petraea)* replaces the English Oak on some light soils and in the mountains of western Europe with a high rainfall: in Britain it is the more common species in the North and West. It is more decorative and a healthier tree than the English Oak, with few galls and regularly lobed, pointed leaves which are more evenly spread over the crown. The branches are generally straighter, less zig-zag. The leaves have much longer stalks but the acorns have very short stalks or none at all. It is also called the Durmast Oak, while the English is often called the Common or Pedunculate Oak. Sessile oakwoods attract redstarts and pied flycatchers.

TURKEY OAK

TURKEY OAK *(Quercus cerris)* is a south European tree much planted well to the north and growing very fast. The bark is dark grey and roughly ridged, the shoots are hairy, and the leaves vary greatly in both length and lobing. Male flowers are dense bunches of greyish-yellow catkins. Note the 'mossy' acorn cup.

HOLM OAK *(Quercus ilex)*, with its Latin name from ◁ the spined, holly-like leaves on young trees, is from the Mediterranean region but is hardy well to the north. It is blackish green all year, except when new leaves emerge in late spring covered in silver hairs. It grows rather slowly and may be bushy.

HOLM OAK **CORK OAK**

CORK OAK *(Quercus suber)* yields in Iberia ordinary cork from its thick bark. It grows quite well in more northern parts, making a spreading big-branched tree. ◁ The undersides of the evergreen leaves are bluish white with dense short hairs. It grows slowly and is rarely 20m tall. The ▷ bole is seldom straight, usually leaning and sinuous, and the lowest limbs may rest on the ground.

53

ENGLISH ELM

54

ENGLISH ELM *(Ulmus procera)* was brought to England in the Iron Age, as a few trees of a local form now unknown elsewhere. The rounded dark leaves are rough above. Small dark red flowers open in February but rarely yield good seed and the tree spreads only by root-suckers.

WYCH ELM *(Ulmus glabra)* is commonest by streams in northern parts and spreads by seeding. The big, broad leaves have very short, densely hairy stalks and are harshly rough above. The fruit hang in bright green bunches before the leaves unfold, then turn brown and fall in June.

CAMPERDOWN ELM (*U.g.* 'Camperdown') comes from a seedling of Wych Elm which was found sprawling on the ground at a Scottish castle. Grafted 2m up on a stem of Wych Elm it grows twisting branches, then hanging shoots reaching the ground all round.

WYCH ELM   CAMPERDOWN ELM

SMOOTH-LEAVED ELM

SMOOTH-LEAVED ELM *(Ulmus carpini-folia)* is the common field elm of Europe: in Britain various forms of it are found in East Anglia. The leaf is smooth and shiny above and the crown has many branches arching out near the top, making a regular large-domed tree. The flowers are out soon after those of the English Elm but the leaves are almost a month later than the English Elm's. The bark is fissured into long vertical ridges. It frequently suckers and bears sprouts on the bole.

CORNISH ELM   WHEATLEY ELM

CORNISH ELM *(U.c.* var. *cornubiensis)* is a Smooth-leafed Elm from NW France with neat, bright shiny green narrow leaves and a distinctive crown. Early settlers brought it to southern Ireland and to England south and west of Dartmoor but no further. Since 1800 it has been planted on a few estates but was rare even before disease killed most of them after 1970.

WHEATLEY ELM *(U.c.* var. *sarniensis)* is the form of Smooth-leafed Elm found on Jersey. It has been much planted in town parks, in avenues and by roadsides for its shapely appearance and its freedom from heavy branches, which can be a danger in other elms. The dark brown bark is broken into square plates as in the English Elm and its broad leaves are also similar to the English Elm, but smooth and shiny above.

TUPELO

Persian Ironwood

TUPELO *(Nyssa sylvatica)* comes from the eastern USA, where they pronounce it 'tooperlow', and has been grown in Europe since before 1750. It needs a rich deep soil to grow at its best and a warm site. In the long sunny autumns of Virginia it shows its brilliant colours in woodland shade, but in less sunny areas full light is needed for the glossy leaves to progress from yellow through orange and scarlet to deep red. The dull grey bark is from early years craggily ridged.

PERSIAN IRONWOOD

SWEET GUM

PERSIAN IRONWOOD *(Parrotia persica)* is usually a broad low tree but often has enough bole to show its flaking bark, orange-brown with yellow patches like a London Plane. The flowers are small dark red tufts open in January.

SWEET GUM *(Liquidambar styraciflua)* from the eastern USA has been widely planted for its splendid and various autumn colours but the summer foliage is also handsome. A crushed leaf has a sweet aroma. The bark is pale grey, deeply ridged.

LONDON PLANE *(Platanus × aceri-folia)* is planted in the streets and parks of every city and may grow rapidly to an immense size. Emerging leaves have soft orange hairs which rub off. Male catkins have small yellow globes of flower and are soon shed. Female flowers are dark red, two to four on each catkin. Bark on young trees flakes away leaving yellow patches.

ORIENTAL PLANE *(Platanus orientalis)* is less robust in cities than is the London Plane, but is equally long-lived and in gardens makes a hugely spreading tree with distinct bronze-purple tints in autumn. The base of the leaf-stalk in planes enfolds the winter-bud. The Oriental Plane is native to the eastern Mediterranean and the Kashmir.

JAPANESE DOUBLE PINK CHERRY (*Prunus* 'Kanzan') is overwhelmingly the commonest of many pink and white spectacular flowering cherries from Japan. It is upright in youth, then the branches arch with increasing age and the weight of blossom. Clusters of thirty or so flowers from six or seven main stalks open bright pink from red buds beneath dark red-brown leaves. They are semi-double with a yellow eye and the petals pale and curl with age.

ERECT JAPANESE CHERRY (*Prunus* 'Amanogawa') is narrowly erect but opens out badly when 7-8m tall. The single or slightly doubled flowers are soft pink and white in big clusters.

JAPANESE CHERRIES

'Kanzan'

'Amanogawa'

WILD CHERRY or GEAN *(Prunus avium)* grows wild in hedgerows and woodland edges on good soils and is commonly planted in parks and gardens. It grows fast but has a rather short life-span. The white single flowers open as the leaves unfold in mid-spring. The tiny cherries, on long stalks, turn from green to red in midsummer and are promptly eaten by blackbirds, thrushes and starlings. In autumn the leaves turn yellow, then dark red.

ALMOND *(Prunus dulcis)*, long brought from the Near East, is common in roads and small gardens. It makes a short, spreading tree with a short life. ▷ The first tree of the season to open large bright pink flowers, it later has heavy dark leaves and big fruit.

WILD CHERRY

ALMOND

63

JAPANESE
CRAB-APPLE

COMMON
PEAR

COMMON PEAR *(Prunus communis)* makes a fairly tall and upright tree in many small gardens. These are cultivated varieties originally raised for their fruit: the wild tree, lower and often spiny, is rarely seen. In winter, pear trees look rather gaunt, with short spurs along the branches; but in mid-spring they are densely set with bunches of white flowers which open before the leaves and last until the leaves are out. The bark is of dark brown square blocks.

JAPANESE CRAB-APPLE *(Malus floribunda)* is very common in gardens, a low, spreading dense tree coming into leaf as early as March. It is quite green in April but crowded with tiny buds which become red. By May these have opened white with pink outer sides, in such numbers as to hide the leaves and the tree is a foaming mass of pink and white. In some years it bears myriads of small fruit, which are usually yellow but sometimes red.

PURPLE CRAB *(Malus × purpurea)* comes in several forms differing slightly in the colour and time of flowering. They are common in streets and small gardens. The one shown here is Eley's Crab, which has the reddest flowers. Out of flower these are all straggly trees with dingy purple-tinged dark leaves, but some hold dark red fruit into the winter. 'Profusion' has its flowers wreathed along the shoots and was deliberately raised to have improved foliage.

PURPLE CRAB

HAWTHORN

ROWAN

HAWTHORN *(Crataegus monogyna)* is a very tough plant growing well on windswept chalk hills and in city parks. Its strong spiny shoots are soon a barrier to cattle, so it is the most used plant for hedges in grazing areas. It withstands constant trimming for hundreds of years but it can still be a tree of 12m. By mid-May every untrimmed plant is massed with white, heavily-scented flowers which leave dark red small fruit or haws. In good years these make the bushes look dark red when the leaves have fallen and are good feed for native and wintering thrushes, blackbirds and waxwings.

ROWAN *(Sorbus aucuparia)* is often called 'Mountain Ash' because its leaves resemble those of the true ash and it grows high on mountains. In wild northern parts its foliage gives the richest autumn red colours. Widely planted in streets and gardens, the fruits colour, in August and are soon eaten by birds.

WHITEBEAM *(Sorbus aria)* shines out amongst other trees on the chalk hills in May when the leaves unfold, covered in silver-white hairs. By midsummer the upper side of the leaf is green. Late in spring the off-white flowers open. The fruit turn scarlet in autumn but are then soon eaten by birds. This tree is much planted together with two selected forms, one narrower, the other with the leaves twice as big, in streets, precincts and parks.

SWEDISH WHITEBEAM *(Sorbus intermedia)* is a sturdy tree with grey scaly bark often planted by roadsides. After emerging covered in grey hairs, the leaves darken and by midsummer are a dull grey-green. It is in the late spring when the tree is most decorative as it flowers in great profusion and then resembles a large hawthorn. The winter shoot is soft pink-grey, purplish towards the tip, and the buds vary from green to dark red-brown but all are covered in short grey hairs. The bark is dull grey with a few long wide fissures.

WHITEBEAM

SWEDISH WHITEBEAM

TREE OF HEAVEN *(Ailanthus altissima)* from northern China thrives in warm cities. The leaves emerge late and bright red, soon turning green but show little autumn colour. When crushed they have a rather stale smell. Male trees have clusters of white flowers. Fruit on female trees are winged and scarlet then remain dull brown after the leaves fall.

HOLLY *(Ilex aquifolium)* grows in oakwoods over most of Europe and may be bushy or a slender, tapering tree. Each tree is either male, with violet tinged small white flowers clustered around the shoots and falling away, or female with smaller flowers ripening to berries. The timber is dense, hard and white, and is used in inlay work. When dried it is a good fuel. Numerous varieties include **'Pyramidalis'** with thick mostly spineless yellowish-green leaves and neat conic crown well berried, and many others with leaf margins yellow or cream. The **Highclere Hollies ('Altaclarensis')** are a group of hybrids with broad, flat few-spined leaves. **'Hodginsii'** a very robust male form with glossy leaves is common in seaside towns and industrial areas.

'Hodginsii'

'Pyramidalis'

Silver-edge

HOLLY

Yellow berries

Common

Yellow-edge

Δ

ROBINIA *(Robinia pseudoacacia)* is the tree, common in cities, often called 'Acacia', while Americans, whose tree it is, refer to it as the locust-tree. The tree soon develops a somewhat craggy appearance, with deeply ridged grey bark and twisting branches. Coming into leaf late and yellow, it is soon a ▷ fresh green after a brief period in some years covered in white, sweetly-scented flowers. The seed-pods hang in brown bunches in autumn. The new shoots have two small spines at the base of each leaf specially notice-able on the often numerous and widespread suckers. The variety 'Frisia', raised in Holland, is now popular, leafing out bright yellow and often keeping its colour until turning orange in autumn but greening considerably in some summers.

'Frisia'

MIMOSA

MIMOSA or **SILVER WATTLE** *(Acacia dealbata)* from Australia can grow as a tree only in southern Europe, SW England and Ireland; further north it needs a south-facing wall. Severe winters inland may cut it back to the ground. The spectacular flowering starts in January in the south while the northernmost trees are out in late April.

71

JUDAS TREE (*Cercis siliquastrum*) comes from the Eastern Mediterranean, and grows and flowers well only in sunny places. It is never more than a low bushy tree, and old branches tend to droop down. The leaves are bluish-green and hairless. The flowers open with or before them, when the tree is bare; the crown becomes dense with flowers, since they are borne not only on small shoots but on branches and even on the bole. The fruit are in flat purplish pods, which remain on the tree well into the winter.

▽

VOSS'S LABURNUM *(Laburnum × watereri)*. The Common and Scotch Laburnums *(L. anagyroides* and *L. alpinum)* were both imported into Britain as ornamental trees centuries ago. Voss's Laburnum is a hybrid between them, and as often happens is superior to either parent; it has the very long tassels of the Scotch and the big flowers closely-set along them of the Common. The poisonous seeds are also less conspicuous and thus less dangerous to children, and this is now the most commonly planted Laburnum. The wood is bright yellow and dark brown.

HONEY-LOCUST *(Gleditsia triacanthos)* is a tough American tree that can thrive among the skyscrapers in every city in that country. In streets a thornless form is usually grown, but in the spiny form the bole bears bunches of branched spines, with new green ones forming each year. The pods are large and twisted, but seen in Britain only after hot summers.

HONEY-LOCUST

LABURNUM

73

SILVER MAPLE

PAPERBARK MAPLE

PAPERBARK MAPLE *(Acer griseum)* sent from SW China in 1901, is seen only in good gardens and parks. Three pale yellow bell-shaped flowers emerge from each bud with the leaves, which are then also yellow. The three leaflets on each leaf soon turn deep green above and blue-white beneath; then, in autumn, they become scarlet and crimson. The peeling bark can be orange or dark red.

SILVER MAPLE *(Acer saccharinum)* from eastern America can grow 1.5m a year when young. Later it has dull red flowers close to the shoots before the leaves unfold. Some boles bear many small sucker shoots. Autumn colours are usually pale yellow or orange. The tree is short-lived but may be 30m tall.

SYCAMORE *(Acer pseudoplatanus)* ranges across Central Europe away from the coast but planted by exposed shores it thrives where others fail. The flowers hang on long catkin-like structures, males towards the tip which is later shed and females near the base remaining to become fruit, which may be scarlet. The seeds sprout like grass almost anywhere and young trees grow very fast. The bark is dark grey until old, when it is in curling orange-brown scales. This tree can live about 400 years.

NORWAY MAPLE *(Acer platanoides)* is wild in much of Europe and planted throughout, often in city streets. The flowers open intense yellow well before the leaves in early spring, and remain, becoming greener, until the leaves are out. The bark is pale grey with shallow ridges and folds. This tree grows fast on acid sands or on chalky soils, and with its large crown turning gold in autumn it is a much valued amenity tree. It is short-lived, seldom surviving more than 150 years.

FIELD MAPLE

RED MAPLE

RED MAPLE *(Acer rubrum)* was sent from eastern America more than 320 years ago but is not common here. It is named from the small bright red flowers, wreathing the shoots in March. Autumn colour is very variable, from yellow through scarlet to purple on different trees. Fruit ripen and are shed early in the summer.

FIELD MAPLE *(Acer campestre)* is native to most of Europe on or near limestone soils. The flowers are yellow-green in bunches rather hidden by the unfolded leaves. Occasionally trees are found 25m tall. Autumn colour is late and bright yellow, turning orange, rarely purple.

HORSE CHESTNUT

HORSE CHESTNUT *(Aesculus hippocastanum)* is native to Greece but is common and seeds itself everywhere. Up to 35m tall, it unfailingly carries thousands of tall panicles of flowers in May. In the autumn a few trees turn scarlet very early and are soon bare, but most turn gold then brown. Some are over 300 years old but others break up and die when half that age.

RED HORSE CHESTNUT *(Aesculus × carnea)* is a hybrid between the European tree and a red-flowered American horse chestnut. The coarse, dark leaves have short-stalked leaflets and the buds are grey-green, the scales edged purple. The flowers in the improved form 'Briotii' shown are bright red but the conkers are quite dull and small, often three to a fruit.

PRIDE OF INDIA *(Koelreuteria paniculata)* from north China grows and flowers best in warm places; the flowers open well after midsummer. The leaves emerge late in spring, bright yellow and turn white before going green. In autumn the fruit, which is inflated, is a bright pink or red.

RED HORSE CHESTNUT

PRIDE OF INDIA

ASH

ASH *(Fraxinus excelsior)* is native to almost all Europe, growing on lime-stones or deep rich valley soils where it can be over 40m tall. It grows fast, matures rapidly and becomes hollow-boled and senile in about 200 years. It is in the Olive family with lilac, privet and forsythia, but this ash has no petals and its flowers are tight bunches of purplish stamens or ovaries, males and females on separate branches or trees. Suckers may be numerous and open their leaves, often tinged purple, before the crown. In the autumn a few trees show yellow, but most shed their leaves while they are still green.

The **Weeping Ash**, 'Pendula', is grafted as high as possible on an ordinary ash and weeps to the ground. Although usually seen grafted at 2-3m up, a few trees are grafted at 15-20m and it has been carried out successfully at 25m.

▽

MANNA ASH

WEEPING ASH

MANNA ASH *(Fraxinus ornus)* comes from the Black Sea region. It is one of the few kinds of ash with petalled and highly fragrant flowers. It makes a domed tree 15-20m tall ▷ covered in slightly creamy white strongly scented flowers in June. It is a good tree for towns and is often planted by main roads. The fruit are very slender, bright green, ripening brown.

LARGE-LEAFED LIME

COMMON LIME

LARGE-LEAFED LIME *(Tilia platyphyllos)* is a native ranging across Europe, known not by size of leaf but by the covering of soft hairs on the shoot, leaf-stalk and veins. It also has larger flowers and fruit than Common and Small-leafed limes, only three or four in a bunch, and the flowers open before those of any other lime.

COMMON LIME *(Tilia × europaea)* is a hybrid between the Large and the Small-Leafed limes. More upright in crown, it can attain 45m in height and is very long-lived.

COMMON
LIME

SMALL-LEAFED
LIME

SMALL-LEAFED LIME *(Tilia cordata)* has neat, small, heart-shaped bright green leaves and numerous small flowers in bunches, which may be erect or hanging at any angle. It has red buds and can be 35m tall, living a long time and often growing many sprouts from burrs.

SILVER LIME *(Tilia tomentosa)* comes from south-eastern Europe and south-western Asia and makes a sturdy, broad tree with a domed crown, which thrives in city parks. The shoot, leaf-stalk and underside of leaf are closely covered in a white felt. The flowers are rich yellow, very fragrant and appear later than those of other limes except the Silver Pendent. The upper surface of the leaf becomes dark, almost blackish green, and the margin is coarsely toothed. The leaves are held out level.

SILVER PENDENT LIME *(Tilia petiolaris)* is not known in the wild and may be a garden form of the Silver Lime. Always seen grafted at 2m on Large-leafed Lime, it has two or three sinuous erect boles and makes a tall, narrow tree to 33m. The leaf-stalk is more slender and longer than in Silver Lime and the smoother, flatter leaves hang from pendulous shoots. It is quite frequent in parks and the larger gardens. The tall crown with hanging outer shoots shows the silvery side of some leaves.

MAGNOLIA *(Magnolia × soulangiana)* is a hybrid between two Chinese magnolias, and was raised in France 160 years ago. A low, broad bushy plant, seldom a tree, it is by far the most common of the magnolias and has given many varieties, differing mainly in the colour of the flower. As in other Asiatic magnolias, the flowers open well before the leaves. Magnolias have some very primitive features, among them a lack of distinction between sepals and petals, so these are together called 'tepals'. The fruit is somewhat like a pine-cone.

CUCUMBER TREE *(Magnolia acuminata)* grows wild from Louisiana to Lake Ontario and makes a shapely, tall tree with a good bole and rich brown bark. As in other American magnolias the flowers open among fully opened leaves and are rather hidden, the more so for being dull yellow-green. After quite rapid early growth the tree lives long but grows slowly. The fruits are somewhat like cucumbers when young.

MAGNOLIA

Cucumber Tree

CUCUMBER TREE

TULIP TREE

TULIP TREE *(Liriodendron tulipifera)* from eastern N. America is in the Magnolia family and in the less cold parts of Europe grows rapidly into a fine specimen tree to 35m tall. The bark is grey in young trees, finely criss-cross ridged becoming warm brown and more coarsely ridged with age. In autumn the leaves turn clear yellow and then orange. A tree is often 20 years or more of age before it starts to flower but old trees are very floriferous and retain the dull brown erect fruit in the winter.

STRAWBERRY TREE *(Arbutus unedo)* is native to the Mediterranean shores and western Ireland and is planted frequently in old gardens in villages. It flowers in late autumn, when the fruit from the previous year ripen scarlet. The fruit can be eaten but has a far from pleasant flavour. The tree is often bushy and rarely 10m tall. The dark red bark of the branches becomes brown and cracked into plates on the bole.

PAULOWNIA

STRAWBERRY TREE

PAULOWNIA *(Paulownia tomentosa)* is native to China but has long been grown in Japan and was sent to Europe first from there in 1838. The smooth grey-barked bole bears rather few, large branches. These are tipped by spikes of small buds through the winter, covered in soft brown hairs. The flowers open in late spring, and are long, trumpet-shaped, pale purplish-blue. The fruit are nearly round, slightly pointed, pale green, glistening and very sticky. The leaves of adult trees are triangular, softly hairy beneath, and often 40cm long. Two-year-old trees can grow 2.5m in one year and bear leaves nearly 1m across with small side lobes. If cut to the ground each time they will do this every year. The Paulownia is short-lived and rarely achieves great size. It needs hot summers, so only flourishes in southerly parts of Europe.

△

INDIAN BEAN TREE *(Catalpa big-nonioides)* comes from just north of the Mississippi delta in the southern U.S.A. It therefore needs hot summers, grows best in the south, and thrives in the heat of cities. It has brown flaky bark and a wide, low crown. It is the last tree to come into leaf. Well after midsummer the flowers open in large heads at the ends of the shoots. Each flower is bell-shaped, short and widely opened, white with purple and orange spots. The fruits are like slender beans, 20cm long.

Indian Bean Tree

1   COAST REDWOOD (page 34) Bark thick, spongy but hard, orange-brown to bright chestnut red especially where frayed; often dark brown and much ridged on oldest trees. Big burrs are sometimes seen, and sprouts are frequent around the base.

2   GIANT SEQUOIA (page 34) Very thick, spongy, soft in parts and flaking and fraying; usually much fluted and ridged, varying from pale brown to dark blackish brown or red-brown.

3   NOBLE FIR (page 16) Smooth and silvery except for a few deep black cracks, becoming dull grey cracked into square blocks, or sometimes dark purple.

4   SERBIAN SPRUCE (page 27) Very flaky orange-brown with some darker flakes and shallow fissures.

5   STONE PINE (page 33) Orange-brown, either pale or dark, smooth long ridges with flaky sides and deep dark brown parallel fissures.

6   MONTEREY PINE (page 30) Young trees dull grey long broad ridges and

6　　　　7　　　　8　　　　9　　　　10

brown fissures; old trees dull grey or purple and brown big flaking ridges and wide, deep fissures; sometimes almost black.

7　CRACK WILLOW (page 36) Soon deeply fissured into network of broad pale brown ridges, darkening with age.

8　GREY POPLAR (page 41) Areas of smooth creamy white with black pits with other parts, especially the base of big trees, dark grey and fissured into prominent small blocks.

9　SWEET CHESTNUT (page 43) Young trees smooth silvery grey with narrow black fissures developing. With age, brown and parallel flat ridges turn increasingly spiral until, when very old, dark brown ridges spiral the tree at a flat angle.

10　SILVER BIRCH (page 45) Young trees dark red and smooth soon flaking to leave white smooth areas gradually marked by diamond-shaped rough areas of black, and at the base, black blocks. Quite large burrs are frequent and may grow sprouts.

11   12   13   14   15

11 BEECH (page 46) Smooth and grey with occasional dark fissures; some trees patterned with pale grey faint ridges criss-crossing, or rippled in patches. Unhealthy trees often have white areas caused by a woolly scale insect.

12 HORNBEAM (page 48) Smooth and pale grey, folded into smooth-sided ribs with dark grey sunken areas, often twisting and patterned with grey lacework.

13 ENGLISH OAK (page 50) At first very smooth brownish then silvery grey. Soon finely fissured into dull grey small plates. When light is suddenly let into a wood, many oaks will grow burrs and sprouts.

14 ENGLISH ELM (page 55) From the first, dark brown, cracked into oblong plates; old tree blackish brown small short-oblong plates. Fine sprouts on small burrs frequent.

15 LONDON PLANE (page 60) Until very big, pale brown with large areas flaked clean, cream, dull yellow, grey-green and brown. Biggest trees dark orange-brown or grey-brown with small parallel ridges and plates.

| 16 | 17 | 18 | 19 | 20 |

16 HONEY-LOCUST (page 73) Dark red-brown or tinged grey with a few small fissures. Spiny form with many clusters of branched and growing spines; unarmed form with sinuous wide fissures scaling coarsely at the edges.

17 PAPERBARK MAPLE (page 74) From the beginning dark orange with big papery scales peeling and in part hanging. Older trees dark red or bright orange-red with big papery scales, leaving clear areas very smooth.

18 HORSE CHESTNUT (page 78) Young trees smooth greenish-grey then grey. Older trees dark orange-brown coarsely scaled, the scales dark, hard and adhering.

19 COMMON LIME (page 82) Grey and smooth at first gradually becoming shallowly ridged in patches and usually growing burrs with big sprouts densely clustered. Deep hollows between the roots run far up the trunk.

20 ASH (page 80) Young trees dull dark grey and smooth. Old trees pale grey regularly networked with flat-topped ridges.

Index of English Names

Index to Scientific Names